The Hierop]
The Star

Ally Wickstead Cummings

The Hierophant And The Star © 2022 Ally Wickstead Cummings

All rights reserved.

No part of this publication may be reproduced, stored in a retrieval system, or transmitted, in any form or by any means, electronic, mechanical, photocopying, recording or otherwise, without the prior written permission of the presenters.

Ally Wickstead Cummings asserts the moral right to be identified as author of this work.

Presentation by *BookLeaf Publishing*

Web: www.bookleafpub.com

E-mail: info@bookleafpub.com

ISBN: 978-93-95890-39-7

First edition 2022

To my darling husband, who has taught me more about grace, humility, strength and love than I ever thought possible. For ever and ever... and a little while longer...

ACKNOWLEDGEMENT

Thanks to my family and friends for their support and encouragement. Particular thanks go to my fellow members of The Writers Coven, without whom I would not have the confidence to have attempted this challenge, and to believe in my work. Special thanks also go to IzzI for the astonishingly beautiful cover photograph.

The Magician

The crowd gasped and cheered in collective glee
as the 'abracadabra-ed' bunny jumped
from the magician's upturned hat.
Squealing and squawking, the children delight in awe,
whilst the cynical adults
with their third eye welded tightly shut
are searching for logic
for meaning
and scientific explanation.
Denying themselves a truth based in
primitive thinking.

A prelogical world
where man and earth were as one;
identical with themselves.
Where mystical
transpersonal
and the unseen
created a weblike psyche,
and archaic man knew magic
was the science of the jungle.

The magician has always been.
Jung's archetype unbound by time,

Untethered by reason, logic and fact.
The wise-person of prehistory
became the philosophers of the ancient world
and the physicists of modern time.
They pull rabbits from hats,
finding explanation to the unexplained.
Archaic, primal thinking
in a 21st century casing.

The High Priestess

In a time when myth, religion and fact
blended into one,
Astarte, mother of the universe,
descended to earth as
a fiery star.

A mother to Desire and Love
and giver of life to all on earth,
offerings of lilies and sweetcakes
adorning statues
stony symbolism of the conceiving womb.

As Hippocrates aligned the humours,
La Papesse brought harmony too:
Ruling over the spirits of the dead
encased in bodies of light
brightening the night sky.

Goddess of fertility, motherhood and war.
Creation and destruction
bound together in eternal dance.
Her image upon card two
vibrating energy and balance.

The Empress

feminine and strong
symbol of fear and desire
conquest? diplomacy

The Emperor

masculine and strong
symbol of awe and control
conquest? dominance

The Hierophant

Lacrateides stood, feet slowly disappearing into the space
where frothy surf meets golden yellow sands,
and they dance together, creating a space
not land and yet not sea.

He looked down at the stone slab in his hands,
engraved with his name.
His lips silently mouthing the letters
as his fingers trace the divots he had carved the night before.

His name was his identity:
his sense of who he was
of who he is.
His calling card for others
and his mark on the annals of time.

But now he has to cast it away
into the depths of the deep cerulean blue
of the Aegean Sea.
Never to be uttered or seen again.

A tear slips from the corner of his eye

as he steps further into the warm, sparkling
water.
With Herculean strength, he lifts his former self
high
and throws him long into the horizon.

The un-named man fell to his knees
Immersing
Purifying
Washing away the last vestiges of life before
and the blueprint of life to be.

He rises to meet his myrtle crown
and gown of purple embroidered cloth;
to carry the Eleusinian Mysteries
and to show the holy to the world.
His name: Hierophant.

The Lovers

To truly love is not
personifying Hallmark inscriptions
Hollywood scripts
or balladlike lyrics.
It is to lie alone in the dark
and feel safe,
encompassed with your lover's warmth.
It is to cry and have your tears wiped
gently away,
and instinctive hands tenderly untying knots
after a hard day.

I know I am loved
and I know I love.
You are my waking thought
and my last at night
as I am yours.

Our love is not beauty and grace
or the glorious tragedy
of Romeo and Juliet.
It is more.
It is you loving me
when I cannot love myself.
Me loving you

when the darkness threatens to fall.
It is reaching out to hold your hand
to kiss your lips
to drown a moment in your eyes
to feel your skin against mine

Loving you has no beginning,
no end.
It is not bound by time
or by earthly restriction,
for I am eternally yours.

The Chariot

Glancing up at the stands
they appeared to take on a life form of their own,
thousands of faces merging to a blur
and individual voices melting into one deafening
roar.

Dread and thrill coursed through his veins in
equal part
As Diocles waited for the countdown to begin.
He knew what he had to do,
he had been through the same yesterday
and would again tomorrow.

He wanted everything that came with the win:
the glory, the fame
to claim Circus Maximus
(nestled between the Aventine and Palatine hills)
as his spiritual home.

Seven laps
each two thousand feet long
the spina bookmarked by hair pin turns.
Every sandy inch accompanied by
three other quadringa in red, yellow and blue.

Gaius Appeulius Diocles:
Hero to thousands of young boys
a true tale of success through adversity
as the child who had nothing
now has it all.

The trumpet sounds!
Dust and hooves fly
as adrenaline courses through his veins,
his muscles reminiscent of those sculpted in marble
are rippling under his sweat glistened skin.

He did not look back as he heard the shattering of wood,
his focus on his own race
all noise had faded to mute.
As his heartbeat matched his horses they were
no longer individual components
but one lithe machine working in unity.

The second blast of trumpet broke through his reverie
And a yell escaped his parched throat
As he realised, he'd won again!

Jumping from the chariot
he ascended to the judges box:

Palm branch, wreath and money were in his arms
and honour was his once again.

Strength

Around the entrance to the chief's hut the men gathered,
calling, clamouring for instruction –
hoping for permission to raise arms
and destroy the enemy.

They could hear the snarling
and clawing of paws against their meagre defences.
Some swearing they could feel the rabid stare
of the hungry, bloodthirsty lion.

For too many days they had been trapped
in a honeypot of their making.
Good men had been lost
to the beast beyond the walls.
No weapon strong enough
to penetrate and destroy.

The crowd fell silent as the chief's daughter
stepped into the sunlight.
Adorned in robe of white
with a belt and crown
of flowers.

Peacefully, she walked to the terracotta mud walls
and stepped through the gate with no hesitation.
The lion, letting out a blood curdling growl
bounded towards his prey.
She stood, resilient and unmoving
as the lion encircled,
biting at her gown.

Slowly she reached out her hand
lightly touching his golden mane.
Running her fingers over his forehead
along his jaw.
The lion felt her strength in every touch,
so taming and calming,
he came quietly to rest at her feet.

The Hermit

"As above, so below"
The words of Hermes Trismegistus
etched into the worn surface
of the Emerald Tablet,
connecting macro and micro
Arabic in hand
Greek in tongue.

Primeval and divine knowledge:
all is created
and pre-existing in God.
And the wisdom of the universe
is a marriage
of alchemy
astrology
and theurgy.

Hermeticism –
where theology and alchemy
are bed fellows
not synonyms for fear.

The Prisca Theologia
that could unite all faith
with God's earliest of words:

echoes of which can be heard
to the ears willing to listen
and know the truth:
One single theology
binds us, one and all.

Wheel Of Fortune

As day brings light to night
Yin balances yang
and peace is a salve for war:
Fortune has it's shadow side.
The wheel always turning,
will it favour the brave
or condemn to a martyr's death?
Sphinx or Anubis –
only fate can decide.

Justice

What is justice?
Another name for karma
where people receive as they deserve?
With trial comes retribution,
but what if retribution precedes trial?
For the innocent bystander of crime:
A life cut short
or the carrier of scars
internal and out,
Justice turns it's head,
and Injustice prevails.

Justice, hear my call!
Do not turn your head in cowardice,
look at the child with no mother
the brother who mourns their sister
the husband with no wife
the father standing above his daughter's grave.
See the pain shining in their eyes
the tears streaking their faces
knuckles white from holding strong
the shuddering of shoulders
wracking with grief.
Where were you Justice?

Where is their justice?
Where was hers?

The Hanged Man

"When you fired the revolver at David Blakely,
what did you intend to do?"
"When I shot him I intended to kill him"

These words echoed and bounced off the walls
of the Old Bailey Court,
morbidly mirroring the sixth bullet that missed
and ricocheted,
wounding a passer by.
His question: her answer; similarly wounding,
but this time delivering a fatal blow.

Fame - perhaps more accurately, infamy – had
finally found Ruth Ellis
with her black suit, white silken blouse and
coiffured Monroe hair
splashed across tabloid and broadsheet;
Far more far reaching than 'uncredited actress'
from Lady Godiva Rides Again.

Twenty minutes,
1,200 seconds
the supposed journey Justice took
from 'how do you do?'
to 'death by hanging'

Subjected to the full medieval savagery of the law*,
without a breath of a pause
to stop and ask 'why'?

Mistrust
Rape
Blackmail
Incest

Miscarriage from a fetal fatal punch

Degradation
Violence
Assault
Mistreatment

Her unspoken reasons why.

*R. Chandler, Evening Standard, 1955

Death

I do not fear death
I fear leaving you.
The pain I know will live
forever in your eyes.
Giving volume to the words
too hard to utter.

The adventures never realised
The jokes yet to tell
The kisses that cannot be shared.

I do not fear memories fading
reducing me to a moss hidden grave stone
or a name on a genealogy tree.
I fear leaving you.
The sense of searching returning
once more to your soul
A never ending journey
to the place that is home.

The secrets we cannot carry together
The burdens upon one shoulder, not two
The stolen cuddles that go untouched.

I do not fear death
I fear leaving you.

Temperance

Huddling further into the upturned woollen
lapels
of his herringbone coat
designed to protect from the brutal icy winds
of New York in winter,
he spat tobacco stained saliva
onto the snow covered side walk beneath his two
tone Oxfords
and swore with frosty frustration.

He knew it was here somewhere
and was increasingly desperate to find
the blind pig.
He needed the warmth
inside and out.
He could almost feel the sweet heat
of moonshine
flowing down his throat
as his eyes rested upon his goal:
The number 21.

He glanced around
looking for signs
of the pure-water army.

Those who felt temperance was not enough,
and abstinence the Godly goal.

He tipped his trilby down to cover
his distinctive, piercing blue eyes
and stepped over the threshold.
"I speak easy, my friend"
he uttered to the doorman,
who nodded him through
into the dimly lit space beyond.

As he settled at the bar
his first glass of the forbidden elixir
appeared wordlessly afore him.
He played with the liquor for a moment
watching it glint against candle light,
sensing the aroma hitting his nostrils.
He picked it up
raising a silent cheer to the
men stood next to women
black folk next to white,
and his lips twitched an ironic smile
at the supposed evils of the world.

The Devil

"10 ounces of gallnuts"
Sweat trickled down the side of my face
sticking my hair to my cold, clammy skin
as I added the first ingredient
marking the beginning of my
Mephistophelian bargain

"3 ounces of roman vitriol"
It had been six days since I first heard
the blood chilling sound of
cloven hoof
upon my flagstone floor,
like an aural Morning Star calling card.

"3 ounces of rock alum"
Avarice was my deadly sin.
My desire for wealth and glory
had eaten away my humanity
and left me skin and bone.
Shades of red, black and blue.

"3 ounces of gum Arabic"
My pact ink was ready:
I was trading the last vestiges of my soul
for the lure of the Diabolo's favour

Mammon
est nomen daemonis*

*Gospel of Saint Luke, The Bible

The Tower

From its heady vantage point atop the Tor
St Michael's Tower stands
surveying the Summerland Meadows below.

Open to the elements, the tower is concrete
rooted
in the shadow of it's older self
having fallen eight hundred years passed
when the land shook with destruction.

The beauty of holiness that once adorned
in decorated floor tile, stained glass windows
and an altar of finest marble,
were now remnants in museum archives
and notations in dusty history books.

As daughter of Glastonbury Abbey,
Christian pilgrims walk the lynchets
in quiet contemplation.

But they also call a different pilgrim
to who walk the three dimensional labyrinth,
as instead of a plinth for crumbling stone
the Tor is the gateway to Avalon
'The Land of the Dead'

and final resting place of King Arthur
and his sweet Guinevere.

The Star

As her eyes settled upon her own image
stretched a dozen storeys high,
she searched for the girl she knew
with her grandmother's words echoing around
her mind,
'Be careful what you wish for'.

She felt a shiver, a stark contrast to
the balmy evening of downtown LA.
She pulled her designer jacket closer
in vain attempt to create substance over style.

The image staring back from buses
magazines
billboards
was a Hollywood dream:
Bette Davis eyes
Marilyn Monroe hair
Rita Hayworth face
in twenty-first century packaging.

She had found the end of her rainbow:
fame, fortune and fancy abounded,
but the ferryman's price had to be paid.

And the girl she knew
she'd never see again.

The Moon

On the fifteenth day
of the eighth month,
as the full moon alights the night sky
casting a fools-day brightness upon earth
Cuội, Chang'e and Jade Rabbit descend
stepping once more
upon the mortal world
for it is Tết Trung Thu.

One fated day,
three thousand years since gone,
a banyan tree sealed Cuội's fate
of eternal life as
the man on the moon.
Not wanting to let go his magic tree
Cuội clung to the roots
and flew beyond the heavens
to his new celestial home.

Here he sits, in the shade of
the leaves, elliptical, glossy and green,
whilst wish-laden lanterns are lit
two hundred thousand miles below.
Upturned faces gaze,
searching for the dark shadows of the

banyan tree.
Seeking for Cuội
in hope for a divine sign
of light and warmth to be reborn.

The Sun

With my eyes screwed tightly shut
I see the sun's image as a shadow,
a burning ball of inky blackness
against the red backdrop of my eyelid

I feel it's heat on my freckly skin
warmth caressing,
massaging flesh and bone
creating beads of sweat upon my brow.

Love is the sun's great metaphor
burning constant and true:
a stark contrast to the inconsistent moon
or ever turning earth.

Our life force of fiery yellow
(a photon present from our past)
an ouroboros unifying man and mankind
yesterday and tomorrow
life and love.

Judgement

With my rainbow hair
almost effervescent in
the midsummer sun,
I am eye-catching.
Curious glances,
blatant stares follow
as I pass on by.
Conservative minds
making assertions
tutting
scowling
at my decorated skin.
Patterns, images
words
sharing, bearing my soul.
Comfort self created
for an uncomfortable body.
Judgements,
foolish indiscretions
and labels
burning, hurting
far more than the needle.
Consider your decisions
and see the woman I am
beneath the rainbow hair

and patterned skin.
And I will invite you:
judge me again.

The World

With a flourish of his wrist
he signed his name
and the world was now his.
He grinned smugly,
revealing a mouth full of gold teeth
decorating his scientifically perfect face.
A result of thousands of hours
of finest surgical craftsmen
commanded to create the uncreatable:
To make him mythical in his beauty.

The teenage footballing genius
had listened to the chanting terraces,
and devoured the tabloid banners
all proclaiming him godlike.
Vanity and desire became him:
His greed insatiable
and goals uncensured.

With the raise of one perfectly sculpted hand
- a living version of David formed
of finest harvested human skin –
He silenced his subjects
and spoke:

"It is as you foretold
I own the world"

Ingram Content Group UK Ltd.
Milton Keynes UK
UKHW021843290523
422528UK00011B/765